Dr. Martin Luther King Jr.

Written by Marcia S. Gresko

Illustrated by Norman Merritt

MARTIN LUTHER KING JR

JAN 15

Why do we remember
Martin Luther King's birthday
each January?

4

Martin Luther King was a
great leader.
He said black people should
be treated the same way as
white people.

5

Dr. Martin Luther King was
a minister.
Dr. King prayed for freedom.
He sang for peace.

Dr. King wanted fair laws
for everyone.
He led marches.
Sometimes he went to jail.

Dr. King gave speeches.
He had a dream that
all people would live together
in friendship and peace.

Dr. Martin Luther King used
peaceful ways to make
changes.
He won the Nobel Prize
for Peace.

Dr. King was killed.
People were sad.
But, his dream is still alive.

How can you help make Dr. King's dream come true?